Warlock Park

And other tales, wonderful and bizarre

by

David Lewis Paget

For my American Muse
Barbara Reiff

Poetry by the same author:
Pen & Ink – the Complete Works 1968 - 2008
Timepieces – Poems Out of Time & Other Places
At Journey's End – Narrative Poems Vol. II
The Demon Horse on the Carousel – and Other Gothic Delights
Poems of Myth & Scare
The Devil on the Tree – and Other Poems of Dysfunction
Tales from the Magi
Taking Root
The Storm and the Tall Ship Pier
The Book on the Topmost Shelf
Tall Tales for Tired Times
Butterflies
The Widow of Martin Black
Goblin Dell
The Mind Catcher
The Angel of Lygon Street
The Obelisk
The Season of the Witch
Smugglers Pie
My China
The Red Knight
Warlock Park

All poems copyright 2017-2019
By David Lewis Paget
All Rights reserved

ISBN – 978-0-6484136-0-8

BARR BOOKS

Poetry Contents

1. Warlock Park 6
2. The Stile 8
3. Spider Bait 11
4. The Poltergeist 15
5. The End of Dream 18
6. Lost Youth 22
7. Death Called My Name 24
8. Raglan Roc 26
9. Love 28
10. Only the Wind 30
11. The Invisible Ship 32
12. The Portent 34
13. Writing 36
14. Starlight 38
15. The Image 40
16. The Widow of Gretchley Green 42
17. The Attempt 46
18. Following the Sage 49
19. Uncle John 51
20. The Bloody Train 53
21. A Tale Will Tell 55
22. Castle McLair 58
23. Christmastime 61
24. Amnesia 63
25. The Ringmaster 67
26. You May Glimpse Wings 70
27. The French Corvette 72
28. The Elopement 74
29. The Selfling 77
30. The Character 79
31. The Lighthouse Wreck 81

32. Moments	84
33. Black Gables	86
34. Birds of a Feather	90
35. The Bones of Arbour Low	93
36. Wolf	96
37. The Chapel	98
38. The Date	101
39. The Lady of Dream	104
40. The Man with the Clockwork Heart	106
41. Raven's Nest	109
42. Kiss of Death	111
43. Barbara Leigh	113
44. Patrolman AI-46	115
45. Skeets	118
46. Fingertips	120
47. Rookwood Nights	122
48. Annabelle Peak	125
49. Blarney	127
50. Days Gone By	130
51. Black and Whites	131
52. The Worst Day	133
53. The Soldier	135
54. Winding the Clock	138
55. Fy Mam	140
56. Dream Sequence	142
57. The Bet	144
58. The Ruling	146
59. The Grimoire	148
60. Death of the Cormorant	150
61. The Thousand Nights	152
62. Time Travel	154
63. Books by the same author	**157**

Foreword

This, my seventeenth volume of narrative poems, is indeed a Park where you may wander at will, as long as you have the intestinal fortitude to do so. In parts of this vast expanse you may feel the hairs on the back of your neck begin to rise for no explicable reason except that you have stumbled across a situation that is alien to you, or outside your previous experience. Pay it no heed. The feeling will go away the moment you close the book.

You may well shudder at times, while reading these tales, especially if you happen to be sitting in a dark room. At the very least, these tales will test your imagination, which is what they're designed to do.

If you're looking for someone to blame, you can pick on my father, god rest him, who placed a copy of Edgar Allan Poe's 'Tales of Mystery and Imagination' in my hands when I was at the tender age of eleven. It was Poe who introduced me to the Gothic, who expanded my imagination in those halcyon days before television arrived to destroy it.

I regard my generation as most fortunate to have partly missed that development, and instead to have had the radio to listen to post-war, when all those breathless serials were coming over the airwaves, and prompting us to imagine what those characters looked like on the other side of the microphone. We were blessed indeed.

David Lewis Paget   April 2019

Warlock Park

It was barely a minute past midnight,
I heard the clatter of hooves,
But not from the echoing cobblestones,
Up on the tiles of roofs,
They came to a halt by my chimney
That belched black smoke in the dark,
As dark as the black caped riders,
The elders of Warlock Park.

They carried the odour of brimstone
That seeped from their capes and hats,
And reeked of additional sulphur,
Embedded in their cravats,
They mumbled between each other
Then gave a blood curdling scream,
That wafted on down my chimney,
'We're looking for Valerie Jean.'

But Valerie Jean lay terrified,
Was hiding under my bed,
I'd taken note of her glaring eyes
Popping right out of her head.
I reached for my trusty shotgun
And stood by the open hearth,
Pointing it up the chimneypiece
And aimed at the one called Garth.

'The first one down gets a double blast
Will send all your bits to Hell,
The next will burn on a griddle plate,
I have got flames, as well.
I haven't got your Valerie Jean,
The one that you call a witch,
She has you conjured under a spell,
You wouldn't know witch from which.'

I heard them grumble in anger then
But climb back onto each horse,
And clatter over my rooftop tiles
Back to their watercourse.
Then Valerie Jean was in my arms
Her tears on me in the dark,
I whispered, 'Conjure your spells and dreams,
But never in Warlock Park.'

The Stile

I always knew there was something strange
About that farmer's stile,
For no-one ever climbed over it
And I'd watched it for a while.
The field beyond it was out of sight
Behind a hawthorn hedge,
I didn't know till I tried to go
It was perched along the edge.

The edge of history, edge of time,
It may have been the gate,
That hell was hidden behind in that
It saved us from our fate,
I threw a stray dog over it first
To see what would transpire,
It came back ravening, racked with thirst
And it set the hedge on fire.

I wasn't going to risk my health
Nor even my sanity,
But somebody else would have to go
For my curiosity.
I passed young Ann in the marketplace
And I thought she'd be no loss,
I talked her into crossing the stile,
She did, at Pentecost.

Now Ann had been unattractive when
I sent her over the stile,
I didn't hear from her straight away
But hung around for a while,
Then out from behind the hawthorn hedge
She suddenly poked her head,
A ravishing beauty Ann was now
When I'd thought she might be dead.

'Could that be possibly you?' I said
When I saw her pouting lips,
Her stylish sash and fluttering lash
And her painted fingertips,
I hadn't noticed her dimples when
I'd looked at her before,
But now she was drop dead gorgeous,
And the word was, 'I adore.'

I tried to get her over the stile
But she said to me, 'No fear,
For everything is so beautiful
I think I'll be staying here.'
And then if I really wanted her
I would have to cross myself,
She said there was gold and rubies there
Amid signs of untold wealth.

I conquered my inner demons and
I took the step at a run,
Leapt over the farmer's stile to Ann,
There in the midday sun,
But all I found was a battleground
Littered with heads and hands,
The rubbish of seven centuries
And a pile of old tin cans.

While Ann was dressed in a peasant gown
And had lost her pouting lips,
Her stylish sash that had turned to ash
And her coarsened fingertips,
'What did you really expect,' she said
As she pinned me to the ground,
'Now you'll be mine, though it seems unkind,
As long as the earth turns round.'

I've tried to escape for seven years
But I cannot find the stile,
The one that I jumped up over once
In response to her woman's wiles.
I really thought I had played the girl
When she wasn't much to see,
But *she* found *me* in the marketplace
And ended up playing *me*...

Spider Bait

I'd seen her wander along the street
A number of times, or more,
And know I should have approached her then
But she might have said, 'what for?'
I could have asked for a date, but then
I left it much too late,
And saw her then with a guy called Ben,
But he looked like spider bait.

He had a straggly beard and hair
That stood up straight in spikes,
I don't know what she could see in him
For my first response was 'Yikes!'
His frame was thin and all caving in
And his clothes were contrabands,
But he clutched at her with a bony paw,
With hair on the back of his hands.

She went to stay at his cottage, which
Was set at the edge of the wood,
More of a tumbledown shack, I thought,
Not right for that neighbourhood.
It lay half-hidden between the trees
With their foliage hanging down,
You had to push past the bushes that
Enclosed the whole surround.

She'd sit out on the verandah with
The sun about to set,
While I would creep in around there
For a glimpse of her, Colette.
I thought, perhaps if she saw me there
She might come out to see,
And once I'd managed to talk to her
She'd fall in love with me.

But Ben would never let go of her
Nor let her out of his sight,
He kept her there by the spiders that
Would weave their webs each night,
From every dangling branch there hung
An orb web in the breeze,
And in each centre a spider that
Would make Colette's blood freeze.

I think he must have been breeding them
He seemed to take delight,
In pointing out how the thousands seemed
To weave there every night,
Then she began to withdraw from him
And refuse his coarse demands,
Whenever he went to reach for her
With his scrawny, hairy hands.

The webs ballooned and they hit the roof
Formed a blanket from the trees,
They covered the little cottage and
I heard her frightened pleas,
She couldn't leave the verandah though
She said that she'd have to go,
He said that he was a spider man,
And that's when I heard his 'No!'

She didn't come out again for days
And I heard her cry at night,
'I hate this place, and I hate your face,'
But he said, 'You're my delight.'
A week went by and I heard her sigh,
The last sound that she made,
So I burst through all the gossamer webs
With an old and rusty blade.

He was knelt beside her form supine
In the corner of the room,
While she was wrapped in gossamer fine
And looked like a large cocoon,
I lashed out with the rusty blade
And cut off his evil head,
When thousands of spiders scurried out
From his neck, and over the bed.

I cut her out of the tight cocoon
And peeled it back from her face,
She hugged me in the gathering gloom
And said, 'Let's leave this place.'
I'd like to say that she went with me
But I'd left my run too late,
'I'll never look at a man again
Since he made me spider bait.'

The Poltergeist

It started late on a Sunday night,
The sudden rattle of pans,
With nobody in the kitchen then,
'What's happening, Dianne?'
Dianne went pale and she looked at me
'You'd better go down and see,
Maybe we have an intruder there,
Just keep him away from me.'

I went, but nobody there of course,
I didn't think there was,
But two large knives on the cupboard were
Arranged in a sort of cross,
'Didn't you put the knives away,'
I called, but she was there,
Looking over my shoulder and
I saw that she was scared.

'But I haven't used those knives for days,
There's something going on,
Somebody must have sneaked in here,
I tell you, this is wrong!'
I turned and I tried to comfort her,
'There's no-one in here now,
Just someone playing a crazy trick,
I'll catch them out, somehow.'

But late that night, in the early hours
The bed began to shake,
Dianne woke up and she grabbed at me,
'I think it's a real earthquake.'
I tumbled onto the floor at that,
But the floor was still and sound,
Only the bed was shaking, quaking,
Just above the ground.

And that was only the start of it,
Strange things went on for weeks,
For things would fly off the table and
Plates off the mantlepiece.
A carving knife pinned me to the wall
By the collar of my shirt,
'I don't think somebody likes you,' said
Dianne, 'you might get hurt.'

Dianne had an ancient father who
Was mean as the day was young,
He hated me, and I used to say,
'How did he stay unhung?'
We rarely went off to visit him
As he acted like a skunk,
But Dianne dragged me along at times
To show a united front.

Doors were slamming and windows cracking
So Dianne had to shout,
'We have to visit my father, Dean,
It's time that we went out.'
I ventured cautiously through his room
And called the old boy's name,
But it was quieter than the tomb
And Dianne said the same.

We found him out in the laundry then,
He'd fallen in the tub,
Had gone a couple of spin cycles,
Oh yes, and here's the rub,
One bony arm and a hand were out
And pointed, looking mean,
We knew then who was the poltergeist,
But boy, his bones were clean.

The End of Dream

They had said that he was dying but
He might as well be home,
He was taking up an empty bed
At the hospital, in Rome,
And no amount of medicaments would
Bring him back to life,
So they threw him in an ambulance
And sent him to his wife.

And she, poor girl, was mystified
She didn't need the stress,
Of tending to a cadaver while
She wore her party dress.
He saw the world through greying eyes
But he never made a sound,
He'd married her through thick and thin
But on thin, she'd let him down.

His days were grey and mist-like as
He looked around his room,
She'd kept the curtains pulled across
So he lay there in the gloom,
And shadows of her sister would
Stand pensive at his bed,
He'd loved, and he really missed her
But the sister long was dead.

Perhaps he should have married Grace
As the younger of the two,
But that would have left the elder one
Not knowing what to do.
The eldest must be married first
Or so the father said,
So Raymond Royce was given no choice
He'd married Gwen instead.

It seemed as if he woke sometimes
And he went to greet the day,
Out in the broader sunshine where
His pains had gone away.
But Gwen was never there with him
As she'd never been in life,
While Grace had sat and talked with him
As if she were alive.

And when Grace reached and held his hand
He thought that his heart would burst,
The tears he shed from his lonely bed
Said he had loved her first.
He asked why Grace had died on him
And she gave him his reply,
'My sister Gwen had put poison in
That gift of an apple pie.'

'She knew I only had eyes for you,
And she thought that you would leave,
She saw the way that you looked at me
And her heart began to grieve.
It wasn't as if she wanted you
But she knew that if you left,
The world would see it as scandal
And would leave her quite bereft.'

And so he lay there, day by day
While his wife brought boyfriends home,
They lay there in the adjoining room
In that little flat in Rome.
While he could not decide between
Reality and dream,
The grey days were his night, he thought
And the brighter days his cream.

He knew just where he would rather be
In the day-like days with Grace,
But Gwen would settle beside his bed
And would mutter to his face.
He saw her dimly through the mist
And repeat beneath her breath,
'How long, how long will you resist
When the end for you is death?'

The day came that the sun was bright,
It was time that he was fed,
While Grace looked on as her sister sat
Beside her husband's bed.
And Grace had whispered between her tears
'Don't you even wonder why…'
While her sister, with a face so grim
Sat and fed him apple pie.

Lost Youth

'I wish that I could be young again,'
He sighed from his easy chair,
Watching the film he'd made back then
When there was still time to spare.
'Why would you want to go back to that,'
His wife said, 'What about me?
We hadn't met when you made that film
Back in 1963.'

Margaret lit an incense stick
And sandalwood filled the air,
A heavy aroma filled the room
As Derek continued to stare.
And there was his wife, at seventeen,
Just walking along the pier,
Should he go up and say hello.
Or should he just disappear?

He suddenly felt so fit, and light,
He hadn't felt that for years,
Then turned to look at his ageing wife
As her eyes all filled with tears.
'You wouldn't pick me again,' she said,
'Not knowing what you know now,'
He would have replied, but love was dead,
Had died, he didn't know how.

'I wouldn't know what I'd do again,
Given the self-same choice,'
'Surely you would,' said Margaret then,
'You would have chosen Joyce.'
He thought of Joyce in the winter barn
As she rolled with him in the hay,
What was the point that she'd said goodbye,
And ended up going away?

'You were still going with Gordon then,'
He said, as if in reply,
'I was surprised that you went with me,
You said that you loved the guy.'
But Margaret's tears were flowing now
And rolling along each cheek,
She should have been true to Gordon, but
He'd gone away for a week.

'Life is just full of ironies,'
He said, while stroking her hair,
'There was a moment, back in time,
When you were suddenly there.
I thought that you cared, and I did too,
We both of us made a choice.'
Too little, too late, to think it now,
For Gordon had married Joyce.

Death Called My Name...

Death called my name, and I replied,
'I'm not quite ready now.
There must be others, more deserving
Of your time, somehow.
I find I still have much to do
Or leave the world in debt,
For instance, all the many women
I've not slept with yet.

'You've followed me for far too long,
I've felt you on my tail,
Your hot breath on my neck, though I
Tried not to leave a trail.
My health is not the best, it's true,
But there are some far worse,
The great decision's up to you
But you should take them first.'

'I noticed when you call my name
There's some disparity,
With other names almost the same
You used a second 't',
Go back and check the register
You'll find some other guy,
Who hides behind my name, he's game,
But you should ask him 'why?''

'You've stalked the world for far too long
In you there's little grace,
You've taken everyone I loved,
You give no breathing space.
Don't worry, I shall let you know
When I am done with life,
Should you want one to practice on
You might try my ex-wife.'

Raglan Roc

Raglan Roc was a Warlock, and
He lived up on Mandrake Hill,
Up where the witches gathered
Once a month, for a coven spell,
He tended his herbal garden, growing
Mugwort, sage and ash,
Supplying the monthly coven, though
He never would deal in cash.

They paid him in philtres, magic charms,
And the odd love potion or two,
For some of the witches were younger ones,
He'd say, 'Let's try it on you.'
And they would giggle and ride their brooms
Right into the witching Dell,
To check out the Warlock's magic wand
As he put them under his spell.

He didn't believe in favourites
But welcomed more than a few,
Till half the coven had buns in the oven
And didn't know what to do.
They got too heavy to ride their brooms
Back down to the village street,
But waddled along the cobblestones,
Tripping over their feet.

And husband's, down in the village square
Would mutter and moan, nonplussed,
'Here comes another, a magic mother,
It should have been one of us.
The place will be full of ankle biters
If this don't come to a stop,
All with a set of tiny horns
And looking like Raglan Roc.'

They followed the witches up the hill
On a coven day in June,
And each one carried a baseball bat
On that sunny afternoon,
They played a tinkling game that day
On his ribs and his Warlock form,
And by the time that they went away
They'd chopped off his favourite horn.

The witches no longer go up the hill
They say it isn't much fun,
Not since the Warlock lost his pants
And his flirting days are done.
They get their herbs from the corner shop
And they weave their spells ad hoc,
While ankle biters still roam the streets
To remind them of Raglan Roc.

Love

To what degree does love survive
No matter what it cost,
Can man escape lost love alive
Once it is truly lost?
When let into a tender heart
Love pierces man's defence,
And leaves the heart with battle scars
Without much recompense.

The early Spring of love will bring
A new and urgent beat,
As love will raise his footsteps up
A foot above the street.
And nature seems to smile on him
From blue, unclouded skies,
The Summer of his love will beam
From her adoring eyes.

But Autumn brings the falling leaves
All dry and burned up, sere,
Once she begins to turn her back
At this time of the year.
Then love will show its darker side
Will threaten to depart,
As he despairs at her grim cares
That tear and shred his heart.

Foul winter is the final stage
When he awakes one day,
To echoes of her footsteps as
He finds she's gone away.
Then life will stretch before him like
A grim, unending storm,
As love will turn its back on him,
He'll wish he'd not been born.

Only The Wind

They laid her out on a plastic sheet
Where she stared unseeingly,
With nothing to cover her naked form
When they said, 'Come in and see.'
I thought how she would be mortified
To be naked under their gaze,
But she was laid in the mortuary
For this was her end of days.

That final humiliation is saved
To be served at the end of life,
They saw her just as an empty shell,
But I, as my loving wife.
She still looked stunning, and had the form
That would peak any man's desire,
But all of life had been ripped and torn
Before she entered the fire.

They'd taken her kidneys, liver too,
And had left some ugly scars,
But her gorgeous breasts, and that little nest
Were left, for they had been ours.
I'd not have shared her with anyone,
We'd sucked at each other's breath,
But she had signed for her organs, so
I had to share her with death.

I heard the crackle of flames behind
The grim steel plate of the door,
That they would open, and thrust her in
Just like a victim of war,
The horror tales of the holocaust
Came flitting across my brain,
That final test that would scorch the flesh
And all I could feel was pain.

She's sitting up on the mantlepiece
In an urn of marble and stone,
A red ribbon sash, surrounding her ash,
I couldn't leave her alone.
I hear her sigh in the early hours
As she did, whenever we sinned,
And wander around our lonely house,
Perhaps, it's only the wind.

The Invisible Ship

Caroline called from the balcony
To join her and check out the bay,
'You wouldn't believe, there's a barquentine,
You never see them today.'
I looked and I scanned the horizon there
But all I could see was the pier,
There wasn't a sign of a barquentine
And all the horizon was clear.

'I can see nothing,' I told her then,
'The sea is as calm as a pond,'
'I'll give you a hint, just make your eyes squint,
Then look to the pier and beyond.'
And suddenly there was a shadow shape,
That looked like a barquentine,
But out where it lay, it was old and grey,
And something about it obscene.

'It makes me uneasy,' I said to her,
'There's something transparent and cold,'
'I think it's romantic,' was her reply,
'It must be two hundred years old.'
It gave me the shivers, I went inside,
As rain pelted in at our door,
Though Caroline wouldn't come in, but sighed,
And stayed where she'd stood before.

That night I woke up in the early hours
To find she had gone from our bed,
I followed her footsteps down to the pier
And saw her just walking ahead.
But Caroline wasn't alone out there
She walked with a man I could see,
And holding his hand, she kissed him, and,
Was as transparent as he.

Then back in the cottage I found her there,
All restless, and tumbled in bed,
She suddenly woke, and gasped as she spoke,
'I've had a strange dream in my head.
I'd been making love in that barquentine
To someone that I never knew,
He said we should go, but I told him 'No',
And then I came looking for you.'

We got up at dawn as the sun came up,
Walked out to the balcony,
We squinted our eyes, but to our surprise,
All we could see was the sea.
There wasn't a sign of that barquentine
But only an empty pier,
And Caroline sighed, stood at my side,
'Some things are much more than queer.'

The Portent

We lived right up on a grassy bluff
That looked down on the sea,
In a tiny cottage, fit for two,
Just Arabelle and me.
But Arabelle was a wistful wraith
Insubstantial in the flesh,
She hovered around in her ghostlike way
With an air of faint distress.

The surrounding air was turbulent
For it always seemed to blow,
Over the top of the bluff from depths
Down in the cove below,
But Arabelle was restless in
Even the faintest breeze,
Worse when the wind came surging up
And swaying the tops of trees.

'Why do you let it get to you,
Why are you so forlorn?'
Often I'd say, as Arabelle
Would sit hunched up, at dawn.
'I can detect a spirit there
That tumbles from out my breath,
That's where the wind is coming from,
It's a portent of death.'

Then she'd begin to gasp for air
As if she couldn't breathe,
I'd say, 'there's plenty of air out there,
It rattles around the eaves,'
I'd take her hand and I'd lead her out
Walking along the bluff,
While she took many a gulp of air
Until she had had enough.

She died quite early one Sunday when
The wind had clattered outside,
I found her slumped on the grassy bluff
From watching the rising tide,
But now, there's only a gentle breeze
Since I've been living alone,
I only hear the clattering gale
When visiting her headstone.

Writing

I'm so heartily sick of writing
As I do most every day,
I'm missing that flash of lightning as
I write my life away.
My friends are dead, or went on ahead
As they left me on the page,
And said, 'You just fill the details in
While we go off to rage.'

I get no sense of achievement from
A page that's white and blank,
I have to fill in some alphabet
Of scenes that I once drank,
I search around for a storyline
That no-one wrote before,
It's like a flea on an elephant,
That's what I'm looking for.

At least I fashion my characters
The way I'd like them be,
The men so brutally strong, and then
The women willowy,
The latter tend to be acrobats
So supple, every night,
And take up a shape impossible
To fill me with delight.

My ladies all are submissive as
They dribble from my pen,
They ask me what I would like to do
And I reply, 'but then…'
I flip through the Kama Sutra for
The inspiration lacked,
And have them jumping through hoops to prove
How well each one is stacked.

But still I'm lacking a storyline
To put my people through,
So I look out of my window just
To watch what folk will do,
The world out there is a scary place
When I look down from above,
The only theme that is not obscene
Is the fairytale of love.

So in the end you can party folks
Go out to roar and rage,
I'd rather be sitting alone and live
Here on the printed page,
It may not be as exciting as
An extra-marital fling,
But I'm content with the themes I'm lent
Because writing is my thing.

Starlight

We had lain back in the meadow
Looking up to see the stars,
They were clustered all together
We were trying to find ours,
For we each had picked a single star
Up in the sky so high,
Then I rolled around to face you
And I found your naked thigh.

They were not among the brightest stars
Up in the sky that night,
But they shone on down upon us
With a pale and pinkish light,
And I wondered why the astral ray
Was pink, and nothing less,
When I realised, reflected was
The tint of naked flesh.

For your dress, it lay unbuttoned,
Was flung open, side to side,
There was nothing left uncovered,
Not your body, nor your pride,
You had never let me see your
Secret places there before,
But you whispered, 'take me gently,
You may enter at the core.'

Now there wasn't but a single inch
Of you but gave me bliss,
Not an inch of pulsing womanhood
I felt I couldn't kiss,
From your ankles to your calves and up
Along each silky thigh,
To that tiny sacred wilderness
That opened to the sky.

I have tasted balm from heaven
From your ankles to your breast,
For your love is all encompassing
I'd not expected less,
And I thank the lord for giving joy
When stars above us shine,
For giving life to womanhood,
And for his grand design.

The Image

I've been looking in the mirror
Every day since I was three,
Till a week ago I looked again
And saw it wasn't me.
For this haggard face with wrinkles
And grey hair that should be black,
Took my place within the mirror,
And it stood there, staring back.

Sure, it registered surprise and seemed
To stare, and be in shock,
And behind me in the mirror stood
Our old grandfather clock,
It was ticking off the moments,
All that I had left of life,
So in case it was an omen, then
I thought I'd call the wife.

'Can you see that ancient visage
In the glass, Penelope?
It's supposed to be my image
But I think it isn't me,'
And Penelope had stood and stared
Then shook her greying hair,
'Yes, that scar was on your left cheek, dear,
But now it isn't there.'

I was staring at the visage and
It gave me quite a fright,
For that scar upon my left cheek now
Showed firmly on the right.
And the parting in my hair was not
Just where it used to be,
For most everything was back to front,
So who the hell was he?

'There's a demon in the mirror,'
I exclaimed, 'it has my mole,
And it's come here from the devil just
To claim my mortal soul,'
So I seized a ball pein hammer and
Attacked the mirror glass,
Till it shattered into tiny shards,
That's seven years, alas!

We've not allowed a mirror in
The house, from then to now,
We won't invite a demon in,
We'll keep him out, somehow.
We know we both are ageing, but
We're not as bad as that,
Penelope will paint her face,
While I just wear a hat.

The Widow of Gretchley Green

I thought that I was the only one
Who had never found a mate,
I'd been so busy with other things
That I'd left it up to fate,
Then I was suddenly fortyish
When I started looking round,
But other people had caught the fish
That were swimming in our town.

The single ones were too young for me,
Their glances all were cold,
Whenever I'd proposition one
They'd say, 'You're much too old.'
And fate had seemingly passed me by
For my early diffidence,
It said, 'you couldn't be bothered,
Now there is no recompense.'

Though most unkind, I became resigned
To my lonely single state,
I thought that whether I lived forever
I'd never get a date,
I'd wander aimlessly round the square
Of my village, Gretchley Green,
And sit alone on the benches there
To watch the passing scene.

I thought I knew every woman there
As they passed, or pushed a pram,
And some went by with their only guy
Or would not know who I am.
But then one day just a yard away
Passed a woman dressed in black,
Her face was covered in net, but then
She turned, was heading back.

She came and sat on the bench by me
And said that her feet were sore,
She'd had to walk from the town hall clock
On some yet unmentioned chore.
I said I'd carry her bag for her
And would see her safely home,
But then I spied her sparkling eyes
As the net on her face was blown.

She didn't look very miserable
For a widow, dressed in black,
But said she'd had a terrible loss,
He'd died of a heart attack.
Though we'd just met, she removed the net
And I saw her dimpled cheeks,
Her hair in clips and her full, red lips
That would haunt my mind for weeks.

She started passing me every day
As I lazed in the village square,
And often sat on the bench with me,
'I thought that I saw you there.'
We'd talk of the trivialities
That you find in village life,
I said that it must be strange for her
As a widow, and not a wife.

I think I must have embarrassed her
So I let the subject drop,
She said she had a confession, but
I told her then to stop.
I wouldn't pry in her private life
Or her deep felt hurt or grief,
She must have loved her departed one,
So I felt like a furtive thief.

She ceased to cover her hair or face
But she still remained in black,
Though wearing more of a jump suit now
Designed for field or track.
It showed her marvellous figure off
And my heart stuck in my throat,
I said if only I'd met her first,
And she said, 'you surely joke.'

It took me weeks to confess my love
When she turned to me, and kissed,
She said, 'I prayed to the lord above,
Now I'm really feeling blessed.
It's hard for me to approach a man
So I had to work a ruse,
I hope that you will forgive my plan…'
But she left me all confused.

'I'd watched from off in the distance
And I really fancied you,
I couldn't come, for it isn't done,
I didn't know what to do.
I'm not a widow at all, you know,
I'll have to make it plain,
The one I lost to a heart attack
Was just my pet Great Dane.'

The Attempt

I'd decided that I'd drown myself
And waded from the shore,
If I had to live without you
I would want to live no more,
For you'd shouted that you'd done with me,
There was no second chance,
Though I'd loved and thought you needed me
You ended our romance.

They had said it was more pleasant than
A gunshot to the chest,
That you'd slowly drift away, and
Wouldn't leave quite such a mess,
And I didn't fancy dying from
A bullet in the head,
It would spoil the later viewing
Even though I would be dead.

I could always cut my throat, I thought,
To make you scream and shout,
For my blood would stain your carpet
You would never get it out,
But I thought it might be painful for
That thirty second bleed,
And at best, I'm quite the coward,
It was pain I didn't need.

So I came in my depression to
The shingle on the shore,
And I watched the massive breakers
As the tide came in once more,
Then it struck me, it was easy
All I had to do was wade,
Way on out to deeper water where
My body could be laid.

I'd be caught by undercurrents,
Taken right out by the rip,
Would be sucked right down and drowned on this
My final deadly trip,
So I pushed on out and waded there,
And pushed against the tide,
Though I wouldn't be quite honest if
I didn't say I cried.

Every time I made a hundred yards
The breakers took me in,
As if the white capped rollers wouldn't
Help me in my sin,
They were thrusting me back shoreward
Every time I tried to turn,
Until I was exhausted
And I found I couldn't drown.

Then I staggered from the water and
I fell upon my face,
And I thought your voice was calling
Till I looked and saw you, Grace,
You were holding out a towel while
You stood and caught your breath,
Then you said, 'Get dry, and come back home,
It's cold, you'll catch your death.'

Following the Sage

You sat in your chair, and read your book,
As often I've seen you do,
While each now and then I'd peek a look,
A glance filled with love for you.
The hour was late, but you didn't stir,
I said I'd be off to bed,
I noticed your look was fixed on your book
So it went right over your head.

I lay awake for an hour or two,
And thought that you might come up,
We'd both had coffee before I came,
I'd made you a second cup,
You may have fallen asleep down there
All cuddled up in your chair,
I cleared my head, and got out of bed,
Thinking to call you there.

I ventured into a darkened lounge
And found that the power had failed,
While lighting flashed through the open blinds,
And thunder above assailed.
But still you sat in your cozy nook
And stared straight down at the page,
Clinging on to your open book
By an old, forgotten sage.

I called you once, and I called you twice
But you didn't move or stir,
I tried to shake you awake, but you
Were cold in the cool night air.
Your face was pale in the flashing light
Of the lightning bursts outside,
And then the terrible truth came out,
You'd sat in your chair, and died.

I tried so hard to revive you, but
You didn't allay my fears,
Your eyes were open, but dull and black,
While my own eyes filled with tears.
I laid your open book on the hearth
And tried to preserve the page,
The final one you were looking at
As you left this mortal stage.

And often now I stare at that book
At the final words you read,
As death crept up and it claimed you then
As those words rang in your head:
'You must let go and come walk with me
To the green fields of the park,
Just take my hand and then leave with me,
Don't be afraid of the dark.'

Uncle John

My Uncle John was a woebegone
In the all out way of things,
Wherever he went, no sun had shone
And we all were ding-a-lings.

He had no time for the hoi poloi
Or women who rant and tweet,
He'd pick on their saddest attributes
When he said they had ugly feet.

But those that he hated most were men
With money, and stick-out ears,
He said they could overhear him when
He whispered to privateers.

When I was a boy, I looked for joy
But he only gave me grief,
He'd say a bloke with a silly joke
Was simply a petty thief.

He'd never praise original thought
He'd say that it sounded dumb,
His wife Elaine said he'd still complain
As long as he sat on his bum.

She once cooked him a glorious meal
He muttered, and spat it out,
So Aunt Elaine said, 'it's such a shame,
I thought it might give him gout.'

I have to tell it was just as well,
He came to a terrible end,
He fell right back with a heart attack
When somebody called him 'friend.'

We planted a bed of chrysanthemums
On his plot in the cemetery,
It gives him something to bitch about
When the cats go there to pee.

The Bloody Train

By a stream of running water,
Underneath a moonless sky,
Like a nightmare of a slaughter
The blood-spattered train goes by.
Where the rails have long been rusted
All along the valley plain,
There the train, so blood encrusted
Will repeat its run again.

I can hear the rails humming
To the rhythm of its wheels,
As the train, it keeps on coming,
As the driver's mind, it reels,
And he stares out through the darkness
With each glaring, bloodshot eye,
He will have to face the horror
When he stops the train, or die.

There's a skull smashed on the boiler,
There's an arm caught on a ledge,
There is blood and guts and gore all spattered,
On the front, and wedged,
When the train ploughed through the gangers who
Were working on the track,
Then their blood sprayed through his cabin
And he didn't dare look back.

Then the fireman had to vomit as
Their blood sprayed in his face,
But he heaped the coals upon it just
To keep their frantic pace,
And now both their eyes are crazy at
The slaughter they have done,
They are bound for hell, not heaven
On this final ghostly run.

It's been sixty seven years now since
That train raced down that track,
And those seven men were slaughtered,
But they keep on coming back,
By a stream of running water,
Underneath a moonless sky,
Like a nightmare of a slaughter
The blood-spattered train goes by.

A Tale Will Tell

He was only a simple storyteller
But looked much like a clown,
He wore red, yellow and jingle bells
When coming to our town,
He'd sit outside by the wishing well
And gather up all the kids,
Who'd laugh, and clap their little hands
At everything he did.

The parents, they didn't like him much,
Their eyes were filled with fear,
They thought, like the Pied Piper, all
Their kids might disappear.
He seemed to be so harmless, though
He won their trust, despite
The stories that he would whisper by
The wishing well each night.

He set up a little pay booth at
The well, and scrawled a sign,
'I only charge but a dollar each
For the stories that are mine.'
But no-one left any money
At his tiny little hut,
So everyone woke one day to find
Their doors were nailed shut.

And then they found in their gardens
There were strange things in the ground,
All their veggies were growing square
That should be growing round,
He told a tale of ungrateful folk
Who proved to be so mean,
Their square was filling with artichokes,
Their lawns were blue, not green.

He asked, would nobody pay him
For his stories and his verse,
They said there wasn't a way in hell,
But he could do his worst,
The beer was turned into water down
At all the local bars,
And when they went to go home, they found
They couldn't start their cars.

They dragged him before a magistrate
Who said, 'You're quite a threat,'
He jingled his bells and said, 'Oh well,
You ain't seen nothing yet.'
The bench the magistrate sat upon
Was wood, cut down from trees,
And suddenly sprouted branches
Five feet high and thick with leaves.

They couldn't admit what he had done,
He'd made them look like fools,
He had a rapport with nature and
He'd modified the rules,
'I've only to tell a story, it
Becomes a new creation,
Anything that I want, I get
From my imagination.'

Everyone pays their dollar now
The streets are neat and clean,
The carrots aren't growing upside down
And even the lawns are green,
But everyone's still suspicious when
It comes to telling tales,
They still remember about their doors
And hide their hammers and nails.

Castle McClair

There wasn't a lot of the Castle left,
A couple of Towers, and Keep,
Most of the walls had fallen in
To a courtyard, full of sheep.
It stood up high on a Scottish hill
Now all enclosed by a farm,
But once there was always blue-blood there,
Brought in by its Highland charm.

It ruled all over the countryside
That it mastered, looking down,
Bolstered by the power of a Laird
With a royal court and a clown,
The Laird was a noble, Ralph McClair,
And his wife, a Lady Ann,
A beauty brought from the Western Isles
But from quite a different clan.

The clown was a kinsman, Rod McBain
Who'd been held from a local feud,
At court he'd been made to entertain
For the peace that his kinsmen sued.
They never ceased to humiliate
McBain for his royal blood,
And dressed him in bells and motley there,
Simply because they could.

From what one knows, as the story goes
When McClair rode far and wide,
Taxing the poorest peasants there
For the sake of his royal pride,
It came one day he returned, they say,
To discover his Lady Ann,
In flagrante delicto in
The arms of a naked man.

The man just happened to be McBain
Who was seized, and his features spoiled,
They ripped the flesh from his back and dropped
Him into a cask of oil,
The oil was heated to boiling point
Till his screams rang out, and loud,
While she was naked, paraded there
In front of the courtyard crowd.

His screams and cries and the lady's sighs
Ate into the castle walls,
And that they say is the only way
To explain the stonework falls,
A fungus grew in the mortar there
And destroyed the Castle McClair,
And as I say, if you go today
You will see the result right there.

For up on that distant Scottish height
You will see the remains of love,
Especially when the Northern Lights
Light up the sky from above,
For stones still fall from the Towers and Keep,
At night, and in winter rain,
And crash down into the courtyard, but
Sounding like screams of pain.

Christmastime

Christmastime was lurking at
The corner of the street,
Just waiting for the 25th.,
It tried to be discreet.
It didn't want to force itself
On Muslims or on Jews,
On atheists, agnostics, or
On skepticism views.

It checked on all the homes that hung
Their holly in the hall,
Dressed up their trees with mistletoe
Hung greetings on the wall.
It wants us to be jolly
It's a giving time of year,
Of gifts of Roses Chocolates,
And cartons full of beer.

For Christmastime is such a gift
To every creed and race,
It doesn't have the time to check
On every scowling face,
For all of those believers it's
The birthday of their Lord,
The one and only saviour
With the favour of his word.

So think on Christmas morning
Of the Lord and of his grace,
Watch emerging little children with
A smile on every face,
And kiss all your beloved ones
Standing by the Christmas tree,
So that Christmas won't be lurking
At the birth of Jesus C.

Amnesia

I came home to an empty house
To find that you were out,
That you'd be home much later, then
I hadn't any doubt,
But the day stretched into evening
Without a sight of you,
And you didn't even call me
Like you always used to do.

When you'd not returned by midnight
I was worried, and was stressed,
I'd thought to call the police, but didn't
Know just what was best,
You might have been embarrassed if
I'd simply jumped the gun,
And you came home unharmed to say:
'I went out, having fun.'

The day stretched into weeks and still
You never came back home,
Though everyone was looking, saying
'Jen's gone off to roam.'
I couldn't quite believe it for
We'd never had a spat,
Some evil had befallen you,
I was so sure of that.

A year went by of heartache but
I hadn't given up,
The house became so lonely when
I had to bite or sup,
To say I cried a river for
A year would understate,
That desolation feeling that
I'd lost my only mate.

And then down on the jetty of
A distant coastal town,
I thought I saw your figure, with
A man, and looking round,
I followed you and caught you
As you got into his car,
But you had simply stared at me,
'I don't know who you are.'

The man was quite aggressive, said
'You're talking to my girl.
You'd better not annoy us, I'll
Reorganise your world,'
I cried, 'Don't you remember me?'
And called her name out, 'Jen,'
She simply stood and stared at me
And said, 'My name is Gwen.'

He dropped you at a hospital,
I'd followed in the rain,
And saw you go inside alone,
While all I felt was pain,
I waited till the man had left
And went in through the door,
Sought out the doctor tending you
Up on the second floor.

He said you had amnesia
Were picked up in the street,
That you had wandered aimlessly
He thought, about a week,
I told him how you'd left one day
And walked out of my life,
And that your name was Jenny, you
Were certainly my wife.

There wasn't much that he could do,
I'd visit every day,
And talk about my life with you,
You'd stare in your dismay,
'My life was just a blank,' you said,
'Before you came along,
But if I can't remember you,
To love you would be wrong.'

I left you there and went back home
But gave you our address,
And hoped that you would call one day,
I couldn't ask for less,
And when you did, your eyes lit up,
'I do remember now,
I'd fallen out of love with you,
And I had to leave somehow.'

The Ringmaster

There were tigers, bears and elephants,
The day that the circus came,
And dwarves and clowns in our tiny town
It never would be the same.
The people stared as it passed on by
It was like a grand parade,
If only we'd known what was going down,
It was time to be afraid.

The tent went up in the open field
Behind old Barney's store,
And lines of booths for the local youths
At a penny or so a draw,
While lines of coloured bulbs lit up
Where the fairground rides were set,
And musical hurdy-gurdies sounded
Just like a passing jet.

Then girls in flimsy bikinis flew
Up and under the top,
A giant net underneath them, yet
In case that one might drop.
The Ringmaster with his hat and whip
And his giant, curled moustache,
Kept all of the bareback riders straight
In line, and under his lash.

The elephants were herded in
And stood on their great hind legs,
Trumpeting sighs, and rolling their eyes,
Just like a dog that begs.
The clowns raced in and disrupted all
Clambering over the seats,
And roused the crowd, that laughed out loud
At all their ridiculous feats.

At ten, the tent had begun to whirl
And the audience went still,
As hounds had bounded in and around,
The Hounds of the Baskervilles.
A massive bell had begun to chime
The Ringmaster's coat turned black,
He grew in size right before their eyes
And some had a heart attack.

He grew two horns on top of his head
That made him look like a goat,
And then a shimmering tail of dread
Slid out, from under his coat.
'You pays yer money and takes yer choice,'
His voice boomed out in a bit,
The prayers prayed and the screamers screamed
As the floor sank into a pit.

The first three rows fell into the pit,
The rest of us stood and cowered,
While he just floated and cracked his whip
Over his pit of power.
And flames shot up from the pit below
To the chime of the Black Mass Bell,
We knew we stood at that terrible hour
By the Seventh Circle of Hell.

Our lips were sealed, and I risk my soul
And any future of grace,
By telling you all just what went down
In this, now devilish place.
You'll see the field behind Barney's store
Lies burnt, still black with their blood,
Where once the Devil's own circus came
And set up in our neighbourhood.

You May Glimpse Wings…

He took to the skies most every night
Unfurling his wings of black, not white,
Invisible in the night sky when
He hovered above the world of men.

'Go out and bring me a virgin girl,'
His master bade from his darkling world,
But scanning this broad humanity
There wasn't a virgin he could see.

He'd scan and swoop from his greater height
When the clouds got into his way at night,
And beam on in to the female kind,
To enter their thoughts, and read each mind.

Then every day he'd return back home
Reporting back where his master roamed,
'There isn't a one,' he said, 'You're sure?
You surely can find me one that's pure.'

'I scan three hundred and more each night,
And none of their thoughts are pearly white,
For even the ones not quite undone
Have dreams that tell them it might be fun.'

'I have to say that they sometimes shock
With dirtier minds than the weathercock,
A virgin body is easy to find,
But not one pure with a virgin mind.'

He still flies out in the midnight world
In a fruitless search for a virgin girl,
Pure in body and pure in mind,
But now extinct in our humankind.

He tells his master his search is cursed,
There's none to find in the universe,
His darkling master is left confused,
'Perhaps you would like one barely used?'

But no, his master will still insist,
And waits in vain for his virgin tryst,
So that's why, under a harvest moon,
You may glimpse wings in the month of June.

The French Corvette

At midnight, out on the cobblestones
There's the sound of rolling wheels,
And a shadow cast on a window pane
From the road outside, it steals,
A wagon, black in its livery,
And pulled by a single horse,
As black as the heart of the man that steers,
Whipped up from the watercourse.

From down in a tiny inlet, deep
Enough for a man of war,
A French corvette is lying, waiting,
Just metres away from shore,
It carried a cargo of brandy, wine,
And cases full of tea,
Smuggled into the tiny cove
Its goods all duty free.

Now it's waiting upon the tide
To turn the ship around,
Its cargo gone in the wagon now,
Headed for higher ground,
And then the galloping hoofbeats echo
Over the cobblestones,
The crack of a couple of pistols and
The air is filled with groans.

The horse breaks free of its halter and
The wagon rolls back down,
It's shadow passing my window pane
A second time around,
It rolls back into the harbour while
I hear the boom of guns,
Firing from the French Corvette
As it hoists its sail, and runs.

Once a year on the fifth of June
And late into the night,
Whenever the moon is lying low
And casting down its light,
I see the shadows and hear the sounds
From that deadly time of yore,
As the ghostly French Corvette departs
And sails from the ghostly shore.

And glistening out on the cobblestones
There's a dampness, looks like mud,
That dissipates in an hour or two,
A pool of the smuggler's blood,
I dare not go to the window, look,
Or even open the door,
In case I'm carried away by them
From two hundred years before.

The Elopement

'Be waiting up at the window,' said
The note he sent by hand,
'I'll come and collect you at midnight,'
Said the note, 'the way we planned.'
She heard the clatter of hoofbeats in
The courtyard down below,
And waved to him from the window
As she seized her portmanteau.

She quickly skipped down the staircase
Holding both her shoes in hand,
Trying to avoid the clatter as
She raced down to her man,
It only took but a moment then
To seat her on his horse,
And gallop out of the courtyard on
Their way to the watercourse.

A light appeared in an upper room
And they heard her father roar,
'By God, you'll pay for your insolence,
I told you once before.'
He'd promised her to a Banker's clerk
Who had paid him for her hand,
Though she had said that it wouldn't work,
She had bowed to his command.

But then the couple had plotted,
He was sworn to break her free,
'If anyone is to marry, it
Will just be you to me.'
They headed down to the water where
The sloop, 'The Esperance',
Was waiting for their arrival
Before sailing off to France.

It took an hour to set the sails
And wait for the tide to turn,
They hid themselves below the deck
In a cabin at the stern,
But soon the thunder of hoofbeats said
They must have been found out,
For then they heard her father's call,
'It's best that you come out,'

He ventured slowly out on the deck
To reason with the man,
Then saw the flash of the powder that
Was loaded in the pan,
The ball cut straight through his windpipe,
Left him sprawling on the deck,
While she was dragged from below, and screamed
'All curses on your neck.'

He locked her into an attic room
And he wouldn't let her out,
Though she would wail, and would scream at him,
And curse and yell, and shout,
She waited up till the early hours
Then she set her room alight,
The fire spread till they all were dead
From that single candlelight.

It sits as a blackened ruin now
With soot on the standing walls,
A testament to a daughter who
Refused to be overruled,
And still some nights when the moon is bright
There's a whisper, close at hand,
'I'll come and collect you at midnight,
And we'll leave, the way we planned.'

The Selfling

I saw her first in the lighting flash
That lit her up in the storm,
The rain was beating on down to slash
Her more than shapely form,
She'd just emerged from a woodland copse
Was soaked as she could be,
So came to shelter beneath the
Mighty Oak, along with me.

Her hair was more than bedraggled, but
As black as a phantom crow,
Her clothes were old and ragged, but
They clung to her figure so,
I asked her what had possessed her then
To wander out in the rain,
She looked at me and began to pout,
'I could well ask you the same.'

I said I wasn't prepared for it,
It came down out of the blue,
Just as the sun went underground
And dark, so what about you?
She said that she only ventured out
When the daylight was eclipsed,
In wind and storm she was newly born
On an evening such as this.

But then she sighed and I saw her eyes
Weren't blue or green, but black,
Her lips an unearthly red, like blood,
No lipstick looked like that.
She said, 'they call me The Selfling, for
I offer myself for free,
I give whatever you want, but then
I take what I want for me.'

She lay down under that mighty tree
And pulled me down on top,
Onto a pile of Autumn leaves,
And said, 'now don't you stop.'
I must confess that I did no less
Than The Selfling said to do,
As she took me into that wilderness
There was pain and pleasure too.

Her teeth bit into my helpless wrist
As we rolled there in the mud,
I felt my essence begin to ebb
As she took a pint of blood.
When I awoke I was on my own
Though I caught a final glimpse,
Of her, in a flash of lightning, though
I've never seen her since.

The Character

I'd got to the final editing
Of my manuscript, last night,
When one of the characters in the gloom
Popped up, he wanted a fight.
'That isn't the way I see myself,
This storyline must cease,
Look at the way you blackened my name,
I'm the villain of the piece.'

'You are what I said you are,' I said,
'Don't bring your complaints to me,
If I'd not written you into the plot
Then you wouldn't even be.'
'You writers are just so arrogant,'
He said, not blinking an eye,
'You make such a mess of people's lives,
And don't even tell them why.'

'I needed a villain,' I replied,
'I thought it best be you,
I don't consult with my characters
When telling them what to do.'
'That's just the point,' said Barry O'Flynn,
'You sign each life away,
So why did you give me an Irish name,
Put me in the I.R.A?'

'You made me a Catholic too,' he said,
'I'm really an atheist,'
'Well, how could I have possibly known?'
He said, 'That's why I'm pissed!
You've made the gorgeous Caroline Cam
Be in love with the hero, Kim,
I don't think he's that much of a man,
So why couldn't I be him?'

Caroline Cam popped up at that
And said, 'It isn't fair,
You've given me that freckly skin
That goes with orange hair!'
I said, 'All right, all bloody right,
I'll let you have your way,
But both of you will totally screw
My plot, whatever I say.'

Now Caroline is a lush brunette
And is going with O'Flynn,
While Kim is in the I.R.A.
And soon will be shooting him.
While Caroline's in the dungeon with
The rats of Castle Clare,
That Kim would once have saved her from,
Now change that, if you dare!

The Lighthouse Wreck

The wreck sat out by the lighthouse where
It lay, smashed up on the rocks,
A miracle it had survived at all
Where felons sat in the stocks.
The bow was sundered, the masts had gone
Long lost in a winter storm,
But still it lay where it lies today
Since before I was even born.

The Lighthouse stands like a monument
But without a single light,
Where once it saved from disaster all
The ships, with its beam at night,
But that was the days of the clipper ships
That would call in from the Cape,
Except for the 'Traveller Grimm' that slipped
On the rocks, and didn't escape.

Those of the crew who didn't drown
Had sworn there wasn't a light,
Nothing to cut through the inky black,
There wasn't a Moon that night,
The first they knew was a grinding crunch
As the keel drove up on the reef,
And then the Lighthouse had loomed on up
From the dark, like a midnight thief.

Often we'd go when the tide was low
Young Jack, and Jenny and me,
Down to the shore where we could explore
Just what was left in the sea.
And then we would climb the Lighthouse stair
Hang out from the very top,
Where once the light had beamed out at night,
Gaze down at the terrible drop.

Then Jack had bet us we couldn't stay
Up there by the light all night,
Without a candle or torch with us
To give us a comforting light,
So up we went in the afternoon
To wait till the sun went down,
Then sat and shivered, there in the gloom,
There was blackness all around.

The sea was muttering round the rocks
Below, till the storm came in,
Then clashed and smashed where the wreck was docked
We seemed to sway with the wind,
The sound came up like the cries of men
Adrift in a cruel sea,
Then Jenny cried, 'that was how they died,
Or that's how it seems to me.'

She climbed up onto the parapet
And swayed there, looking down,
And Jack said that he would join her there,
While I held back, and frowned.
The two were standing and holding hands
When Jenny tripped on the ledge,
So when she toppled, she took him down,
While I just clung to the edge.

I heard them hit on the 'Traveller Grimm',
On what was left of the deck.
They both had died from a stupid whim,
As both had a broken neck.
I never went back to that Lighthouse stair,
They sealed it up, like a tomb,
Then put up a sign that said 'Beware',
That glows at night in the gloom.

Moments

Words flutter by us,
Caught in their moments,
Words sent to try us,
'Loss' and 'Elopements',
Some may inspire us,
Others may burn,
Once they decry us
They never return

Some were left out there,
When I was young,
Caught in the frost where
My youth was undone.
Some may pass by me
More often, and then,
Echo in silence and
Drip from my pen.

Where do they float to,
That is the mystery,
Some learnt by rote to
Be writ in each history,
Others elude us but
Catch at our breath,
Slide in our coffins and
Hound us to death.

While we are ever
Living and breathing,
Some words should never
Be heard, one is 'Leaving',
Three words are only
Both honest and true,
Should one be left lonely,
And those, 'I love you.'

Black Gables

The house had heavy gables that
Had once been painted black,
Though now weathered and distempered
In assaulting time's attack,
But it had a certain charm that drew me
Up to the front door,
Where a notice said, 'For Sale or Rent,
Just knock, and ask for more.'

So I reached up for the knocker that
Was dark and oddly shaped,
Like the visage of a goat's head
That from Hell must have escaped,
For the horns were grim and twisted
And the eyes gleamed in the dark,
Like two beams that saw right through me
Staring out towards the park.

Then I rapped the knocker on the plate
Three times, or maybe more,
Till I heard the sound of shuffling
Two feet behind the door,
And I heard the rasp of rusty bolts
Someone was drawing back,
When the door began to open with
A creak, and then a crack.

Then a woman stood before me
Peering out through tangled hair,
In an old and tattered dust coat
With a look that said, 'despair',
But she stood aside to wave me in
Then muttered rather low,
'You're here at last, you should have come
Some twenty years ago.'

I stood there quite bewildered in
The shadows of that hall,
And I fancied shades were dancing,
Painting patterns on the wall,
But she led me to a room that glowed
In eerie candlelight,
And she sat me at a table as
The day fled into night.

'Do you want to rent or buy it?'
Was the next thing that she said,
In a voice that creaked of ages lost
In some almighty dread,
So I said I'd like to rent it if
It wasn't very dear,
She replied, 'A golden guinea will
Suffice, for half a year.'

Then she placed the lease before me,
And she brushed away the dust,
For the lease must have been lying while
The knocker turned to rust,
And a feather quill was standing in
A vase, all stained with mud,
'There's just one thing,' she ventured,
'You must sign the lease in blood.'

I sat back in shock and horror
And I said, that wouldn't do,
My blood was all accounted for,
'I'll not do that for you.'
She took a cut throat razor from
A pocket, with a twist,
Then turned to me and said, 'you see,'
And swiftly slashed her wrist.

She dipped the quill and twisted it
To soak the tip in blood,
Then thrust it in my open hand
And said, 'you really should,'
But I shrank back to get away
From this godawful crone,
And screamed, 'I think I've changed my mind,
You must leave me alone.'

I ran back to the passageway
With her hard up behind,
She screamed 'you mustn't leave me now,
I've almost lost my mind.
I've waited twenty years for you
To come and rescue me,
This house has owned my very soul,
I just want to be free.'

I took the pathway at a run
Not daring to look back,
But heard a scream like some dark dream
As I ran down that track,
And in the gloom I heard the creak
Of hinges, on that door,
And then it slammed, and she was trapped
In there, forevermore.

Birds of a Feather

I have always been unstable
Since that day in fifty-three
When a bolt of lightning lit me
In that poor old acorn tree,
When the tree split down the middle
Taking my half to the ground,
And that clap of awful thunder
Left me lying, with no sound.

I was dazed and fazed and humbled
In a new but silent world,
While my brain had seemed to tumble
As my mind and vision whirled,
I could see a host of demons
Grinning down and mocking me,
From the topmost of the branches
That remained, within that tree.

While my hearing soon recovered
I was suffering from shock,
And could hear the voices whispering
Behind the mantle clock,
And I'd catch a glimpse of shadows
At the corner of each eye,
As they whispered, 'Did we get him,' and,
'Is he about to die?'

So I grew up feeling paranoid
For others couldn't see,
All the movements in the shadows
That were now surrounding me,
And they couldn't hear the whispers
In the pillow as I slept,
That would tease and taunt, torment me
Till I woke, and sat and wept.

Then I made a friend called Jenny
Who had issues of her own,
She'd burnt out her brain on acid
Till her wits and mind had flown,
We were two birds of a feather
As we huddled in our den,
And exchanged our sights and whispers
From beyond the world of men.

But I thanked the lord for Jenny
For his largesse from above,
Though her pound was like a penny
Still, I think I fell in love,
We could manage all our demons
If we held each other tight,
Though our oranges were lemons
We still made love every night.

We would often go out walking
In the country for the air,
Although still our shades and whispers, they
Would follow us out there,
Then beside an old canal one day
The water sparkled bright.
And Jenny stood transfigured at
That awesome, magic sight.

'I think I'll walk on water,' was
The last thing that she said,
Then stepping off the towpath in
A moment, she was dead,
I reached, and tried to reel her in
By tugging at her hair,
But she remained face down, and left me
Deep in my despair.

My voices have deserted me,
My shades, they never come,
I sit here in my silent world
Ignoring everyone,
They say it's shock and horror
That has put me in this trance,
My mind is full of Jenny now
And all we do is dance.

The Bones of Arbour Low

The mansion known as Arbour Low
Came to me in a will,
From someone called Great Uncle George,
I'd never met him, still,
I'd heard he was so miserly
He'd thrown his sister out,
And beaten his poor wife, I heard,
He truly was a lout.

He lived alone in that great house
Long after Rachel died,
Would never admit visitors
But hid himself inside,
He had one friend, a single friend
Who always stuck by him,
But disappeared one August night
Was never seen again.

The house was dark and gloomy, lit
By candles in each room,
It didn't have electric power
To lighten up the gloom,
The rooms were full of cobwebs, and
Thick dust was everywhere,
And every room smelt foetid,
It was hard to breathe in there.

I cleaned it up as best I could,
Used only rooms below,
I didn't venture up the stairs,
I didn't want to go.
It seemed so dark, foreboding that
The thing I felt was fright,
When staring up that darkness pit,
The stairway, every night.

I wondered about George's friend,
The one who'd disappeared,
Could he have died in this old house?
That was the thing I feared,
They said he'd come to visit George
This one and only friend,
But once that door slammed shut on him
He wasn't seen again.

The house was old, and worn, and sad,
At night the stairs would creak,
I lay below stretched on a couch
But often couldn't sleep,
A friend of mine who read the cards
Brought round her crystal ball,
And said to hold a seance there
One night there, in the Fall.

'If there are secrets in this house,
The crystal finds them out,
That man who disappeared, his name
Was Hugo Where, no doubt.'
She laughed and joked, and read the cards,
Stared at the crystal ball,
And called his name right up the stairs,
It echoed off the wall.

At midnight she had done her best
And said, 'I'm giving in,
The shadows in the crystal ball
Foretell of some deep sin.'
Then in the darkness came a sound,
That saw us both undone,
For stumbling down the stairway came
A rattling skeleton.

Wolf

Lock the shutters and pull the blinds
And set up the alarm,
Chain the dogs up safe, and lock
The chickens in the barn,
The sun has sunk beneath the ridge
The Moon is riding high,
And casting its cold evil beam
From a cold and evil sky.

The Wolf's been seen in Basingdene,
Roamed through the Southern Vales,
It's come into our county from
Its den, somewhere in Wales,
Bring up the sheep into the pen
And break my rifle out,
I'll watch for it all night until
Its shadow leaves no doubt.

The night is long and lonely and
The air's becoming chill,
I thought I saw a shadow move
Up over on the hill,
Its coat is black as deepest night
Its eyes a yellow glint,
With teeth so white and sharp, they gleam,
And give the slightest hint.

The hedge will keep the Wolf at bay
Up to the farmyard gate,
Then it might try to slip on through
And there will meet its fate.
It won't be like the time before
When Alice screamed a note,
Caught walking in the pasture as
The Wolf tore at her throat.

The Moon is full, and round and white
And lights the farmyard gate,
I watch the black coat slinking in
And all I feel is hate.
It halts, to sniff the air, and howl
While I line up the sight,
And blast it through its yellow eye
On this revengeful night.

The Chapel

The road was a-twist and turning
As I crested the mountainside,
The sun in my eyes was burning
Then it set on the hills, and died,
The night had settled into a gloom
As the moon rose up from the sea,
And then in the dark, an ancient tomb
Appeared in front of me.

It stood in the grounds of a chapel
That was ruined and empty now,
I stopped and I ate an apple,
To quench my thirst, somehow,
I parked the car by the chapel gate
And ventured to look around,
When by the light of a flimsy torch
I caught at my breath, and frowned.

The name on the tomb was Tangell Garth
An inscription said below,
'He lived when the giants roamed the earth
Till the Floods had laid them low',
And there on the top stood a mighty skull
With a long, extended dome,
I thought it was sculptured, till I looked
And saw it was made of bone.

Its eyes were the size of dinner plates
Its jaw like a dinosaur,
With teeth for ripping and tearing like
Had never been seen before,
A bitter breeze then began to blow
And soon it began to rain,
I sheltered then in the chapel,
Before hitting the road again.

The chapel walls were of mud and stone
With the roof part fallen in,
A smell rose up from the bracken floor
Like some odour of ancient sin,
But by the altar a graven beast
That must have been ten feet high,
Stood scowling down like the skull I'd found
On the terrible tomb outside.

And on the altar were running stains
That first I had thought were mud,
Until I had shone the torch on them,
And then I could see, were blood.
Such ancient stains sunk into the stone
They never could wash away,
As terror entered my very bones,
I needed to get away.

Then lightning flashed in the evening sky
And lit up the graven beast,
For just a moment, suddenly I
Was there when it came to feast,
A ghostly girl on the altar screamed
As a blade ripped through her throat,
And blood dripped out of the sculpture's mouth
From a thousand years, at most.

I ran headlong from that chapel as
The thing began to roar,
While thunder crashed and the lightning flashed,
I ran to my waiting car,
I've looked in vain for that place again
When the sun was bright and high,
But never remained when night would reign
For fear that I'd surely die.

The Date

The girl popped up on my Messenger
And said, 'Do you want to date?'
I said, 'I think I'm too old for you,
You've left it a little late.'
'I don't think age is a problem,' she
Replied on the silver screen,
'I'll meet you down at the Horse and Hound
Then you can see what I mean.'

I must admit I was curious
So ran a comb through my hair,
At least, what little was left of it
There wasn't a lot to spare,
I wondered what she had seen in me
But soon I was outward bound,
Driving the mile through Oswestry
To meet at the Horse and Hound.

She sat alone at a table there
And smiled as I wandered in,
She must have been all of thirty-three
With a smile as wicked as sin.
She told me her name was Erika
And that she felt drawn to me,
Told me she'd lived in Africa
Though was pale as pale could be.

I said I was much too old for her
Though I thought her really nice,
She reached on out and she held my hand
But her hand was cold as ice,
Her skin was smoother than marble
And her eyes were crystal blue,
Her gaze was fierce as they filled with tears,
She said, 'I just want you.'

We ended back at her flat, somehow,
Of African charms and tokens,
Carved wooden heads strung across her bed
And a totem that was broken,
She sat me down with a bushman's hat
And she cooked a vile concoction,
I asked her where she had got the stuff,
'I bought it all at auction.'

Then she poured me a brimming cup
And bid me then to drink it,
She begged me, saying 'My time is short',
I had no time to think it.
A sip was all I could take, it had
The taste of flavoured mud,
She flung herself on my neck, and said
'I need a pint of blood.'

I pushed the woman away, she fell
To crouching in the corner,
And crying that I would go to hell
If I'd not become her donor,
Then she shrivelled, that perfect skin
Was cracked and aged like parchment,
She lay, a hundred and fifty three
At least, in that apartment.

So now I'm wary of Messenger
And of women that approach me,
I won't take younger than sixty three
If a woman wants to coach me,
If once they say that age doesn't count
I break out in a sweat,
And say, 'so sorry, I'm married now,'
And I haven't met one yet.

The Lady of Dream

She lived tucked away in a tiny room,
With a simple computer screen,
A table, a bed, and dreams in her head
Of how once the world had been.
She'd not venture out, her life was a drought
Since the love of her life had died,
Though men came to court, that's not what she sought,
This lady had too much pride.

She felt she could not fall in love again,
That pain was too hard to bear,
She'd savoured the best, and so for the rest
She lived like she wasn't there.
Her children were grown, so mostly alone,
Her days went un-noticed, and flew,
Resigned to her age, she didn't engage
With a world that she barely knew.

I saw her just briefly pop up on my screen,
A whisper, and then she was gone,
A tangle of hair, and cheeks that were fair,
And eyes that had fairly shone.
I felt something stirring inside of me then
Like an angel had passed my way,
A simple respite in the depths of the night
That carried on into the day.

I sought and I searched for the vision I'd seen,
In the hopes that she'd soon be there,
For day after day, I'd look for a way
To find her, induce her to care.
My life had been empty, my heart ceased to beat
Till I saw her face up on the screen,
But then it awoke at the first time I spoke
To that wonderful Lady of Dream.

I know it takes time, to make love online,
But time is the one thing we had,
And both of us find, we're of a like mind
In all things both happy and sad.
There may be an ocean between her and I
But you're only as close as you feel,
And so it would seem, when the Lady of Dream
Reaches out, then the feeling is real.

The Man with the Clockwork Heart

'Emmanuel's heart is beginning to fail,'
They said to his doting wife,
'That's why he's having these fainting spells,
He's at the end of his life.'
'But why can't you give him a brand new heart?'
She wept, at the awful news,
'There isn't the cover to cover your lover,
So tell him or not, you choose.'

She chose to keep it a secret then,
But sought out another quack,
She wanted a second opinion,
A more positive one than that.
He told her it was expensive, but
He knew of a cheaper part,
If she would agree to a minimal fee
He'd fit him a clockwork heart.

'You'll have to wind it up twice a day
With a key you'll fit in his back,
But don't forget or you might regret
And he'll suffer a heart attack.'
She said she knew, and she fairly flew
As she set out, heading home,
And told Emmanuel, he must go
With her, to the doctor's room.

She never told him what she had done,
But wound him up with the key,
Twice a day while asleep he lay
Or napping across her knee.
He said he felt full of energy
For the first time then, in years,
And they would play as in bed they lay
While her eyes would fill with tears.

He said when he lay awake at night
He could hear a tick like a clock,
And when it wasn't a tick he heard
He could swear it was a tock.
'It's just the clock in the hallway, dear,'
She said, to calm his fears,
And made him a balaclava then
To cover up his ears.

She wouldn't let him go swimming
Just in case the spring would rust,
And kept the key in a secret place
Up high, where she didn't dust,
She always set the alarm for when
She knew she'd have to wind,
He thought it simply a quirk of hers,
She used it to remind.

One day, she found he was missing in
The middle of the day,
He'd taken off for a walk, forgot
To tell his wife which way,
She madly ran round the neighbourhood
While clutching tight the key,
But couldn't see where he'd gone
It seemed to be a mystery.

They found him slumped on the footpath
And she had to cart him home,
He wasn't moving a muscle so
She knew she was alone,
She wound until he was ticking
But her husband didn't start,
There's no repair for a lover, or
A Man with a Clockwork Heart.

Raven's Nest

She lived at the top of Raven's Nest
So I was determined to go,
To seek out the sunny uplands there
Where the four fair winds do blow,
To seek out the breeze at the top of the trees
That carry the sun-drenched dew,
While up on the topmost battlements
I'd get a brief glimpse of you.

The lady that walked in her deepest sleep
They said, till her love came true,
The tenderest kiss at her greying lips
Would give them a rose red hue,
The charm that had put her to sleep would lift
The veil from her opaque eyes,
Revealing the view of a vivid blue,
Unleashing her wondrous sighs.

The battlements there are grey and bleak
A prison for all delight,
While up on the height, the Raven's beak
Looks out, to sully the night.
It flutters its wings like a guardian
At any who climb and approach
That lady's rest, up at Raven's Nest,
To deter, arrest, reproach.

I chose the night of a Harvest Moon
To attempt my one desire,
Taking a dart and a crossbow there
With a flint for a mighty fire.
The Raven fluttered as I approached
And I shot it through the heart,
Then it fell away in its bleak dismay
In the fire of my flaming dart.

The lady walked at the battlements
And I tugged at her holy gown,
She stopped and stared, as if she was scared
In her sleep, she looked and frowned.
I kissed her tempting, greying lips
And they turned to a rose red hue,
As I breathed, 'My love.' From heaven above
She said, 'I was waiting for you.'

Kiss of Death

'Why have you left me here, alone,'
She said with a tearful eye,
And stared at the the cold and grey headstone
Expecting a cold reply.
The breeze above just rustled the leaves
Of the tree above the grave,
And seemed to say, in its wayward way,
'There was nothing left to save.'

'Whatever we had was old and spent
When you turned to another man,
And walked in the park when the sky was dark,
Allowed him to hold your hand.
I happened along the old towpath
So your form I couldn't miss,
And felt the breath of a kind of death
As you both leaned in, to kiss.'

The boughs of the tree then caught the breeze
Swayed low, and they then unbent,
Reaching on high, to stare at the sky
As the hurt in her cry was rent.
'I never went for a walk in the park,
That night I was staying in,
You couldn't have seen what never has been,
So what you saw was my twin.'

The thunder rumbled up in the sky
And mumbled its discontent,
As lightning shattered the grey headstone
When she turned away, and went.
A bough broke off, and fell to the ground
Where a cringing shadow crept,
As she walked alone to an empty home
And the weeping willow wept.

Barbara Leigh

The news came via the telephone,
'You must come on home at once,'
The voice had rasped with an urgent tone
As if talking to a dunce.
He wouldn't say what was going on
He just said, 'Come home and see,'
My heart had fluttered before I uttered
'What's up with Barbara Leigh?'

I held my breath as I heard the click
When he put the handset down,
And breathed a curse just under my breath
As I called the fool a clown.
He knew that I'd be worried sick
When he left me up in the air,
It could only be that Barbara Leigh
Was hurt, or in despair.

I knew full well that he hated me
Because of his blighted love,
He'd made it plain that Barbara Leigh
Should be his, from heaven above,
But she'd turned her graceful smile on me
And had left him in the lurch,
And the only time he saw her was
When we married, in the church.

I had to drive three hundred miles
To get home to Barbara Leigh,
And had bitten through my bottom lip
As I counted every tree,
I felt the tears course down my cheek
As imagination bled,
And thought through every scenario
That I'd find my lover dead.

For hour on hour the road sped by
And the daylight fled to night,
My headlight beams, they were lost in dreams
Of the one, my one delight,
My hands were shaking so badly
When I pulled into our drive,
Until I saw, and was hoping for
That my Barbara was alive.

She rushed on out of the cottage door
With one of her winning smiles,
I said, 'By God,' with relief, a nod,
'I've just raced three hundred miles!'
'I didn't want to distress you, love,'
But her face was creased with joy,
'I simply wanted to tell you first,
We're having a baby boy.'

Patrolman AI-46

The policeman pulled me over but
He wouldn't tell me why,
He kept his visor closed so there
Was never eye to eye,
He wore that riot police gear like
Black armour, head to toe,
And muttered through his helmet
'Just this once, I'll let you go.'

I sat there quite bemused and said
'What is it that I've done?
I've followed all the traffic rules,
Not broken even one.'
He growled, and slapped my window with
His black-like gauntlet glove,
'You'd better hold your tongue or
There'll be vengeance, from above.'

'I don't quite understand,' I said,
Not leaving it alone,
I felt a growing grievance for
This dark, unthinking drone,
'You've pulled me up for nothing,
Not a thing, for nothing, nix,
I think I'll take your number,'
He said 'AI-46.'

And then he pulled his taser,
I began to be alarmed,
And wound right up my window,
Hoped to keep myself from harm,
His hand was jammed in tight
Between the window and the door,
And then he dropped his taser
Right inside, down on the floor.

I freaked, and jammed my foot down
On the pedal, not the brake,
The car shot ten feet forward
Dragging him along its wake,
His helmet started beeping with
A sound of great distress,
As the car ripped off his arm between
His shoulder and his chest.

He fell into the road and then
His helmet flew ahead,
It rolled along the road and I
Was sure that he was dead,
Still the helmet lay there empty
But for coils and loops of wire,
And computer bits and circuits that
Sparked once, then caught on fire.

I looked for blood and gore but there
Was only bits of mesh,
That riot suit was empty, didn't
Hold blood, bone or flesh,
But somewhere in that headless suit
A voice repeated licks,
Of audio that said again
'I'm AI-46.'

A sergeant came patrolling and
Looked down and kicked the suit,
'It's said to be intelligent,
Not fit for picking fruit.
They say that they'll replace us,
On the beat, out in the Styx,'
The empty suit replied again
'I'm AI-46.'

Skeets

I used to play in a Grotto
Right next to a deep lagoon,
Hidden among the wing-wang trees
Most every afternoon,
The reeds were teeming with scuttle-bucks
And furry galloping skeets,
But often the rambling wangle-wox
Wouldn't be seen for weeks.

Deep in the shallow waters,
They'd frisk, and frug and play,
Almost every day of the week
Except for Saturday,
The watercress was a shade of kew
And the shlubs a vivid skeen,
Trailing into the water globes
As if their leaks were green.

I'd lie on the lank forget-me-nots
And while away the day,
Hoping to see the wangle-wox
Disport, and frug and play,
And often I'd wake to find I lay
Next to the crocodile,
That slithered up from the cool lagoon
To sun itself for a while.

But then I found I was almost ten
And the blue lagoon a pond,
The wing-wang trees drooped in the breeze
With a weeping willow frond,
The scuttle-bucks were Muscovy ducks
And the wox a feral fox,
But still I miss the galloping skeets
And the sleepy lizard crocs.

Fingertips

Remember that day at the edge of the cliff
Where the path slopes steeply down?
Holding your hand in the loosening grip
Of your endless, tardy frown,
Nothing I said would lighten your mood,
Nothing would make you smile,
All of our history, hidden in mist
For the last long mile.

Every misfortune affected the love
That you had in your heart for me,
Though I had prayed to the heavens above
It was not, or never to be.
Every reverse had blighted our lives,
Fate left our wishes spurned,
You said that the blame attached to my name
Was all that I really earned.

But you were the one invading my heart,
I held that invader still,
I'd never let go of the love that I know
My life was meant to fulfil,
I could feel you slipping away from me,
Was facing a downward flight,
If you should go, I want you to know
You'd leave me in endless night.

But then that day on the downward path
Right on the edge of the cliff,
The shale dislodged, and tripping us down
We hung by our fingertips,
I turned, and clinging so tight to you,
There was no sign of your frown,
But rather a look of wonderment
As I noticed you, looking down.

Right at the edge of that precipice
You said that you realised
That what you had was too good to miss,
You saw the love in my eyes.
From that day on I've enjoyed your lips
Whatever our fate has tossed,,
While clinging on by our fingertips
To the love that we almost lost.

Rookwood Nights

I used to love my Rookwood nights
When my friends and I would meet,
We'd gather together as birds of a feather
Joanne, Martin and Pete,
Then into the darkening woods we'd go
With our sturdy, children's legs,
Ready to climb to the top of the trees,
Looking for Rookery eggs.

The rooks would nest in the tallest trees
And would lay their eggs blue-green,
With spots of brown on the eggs, all round,
Where the tallest trees were seen,
We'd look for the ash, the beech, the oak,
And the chestnut trees for signs,
For bunches of nests in the sycamore trees
Stood out against the skies.

The challenge for us to climb to the top
Left us scratched and bleeding legs,
But nothing would quell our excitement
When we clambered in search of eggs,
A rook's egg was a rarity
For they were so hard to find,
Too far above where the boughs would bend,
And break with children kind.

Pete would stick to the royal oak
While I preferred the ash,
Joanne shinned up the sycamore trees
While Martin kept the stash.
He'd catch the eggs as we threw them down
And he'd rarely miss a one,
A single egg was the price we sought
For each and everyone.

One night a cry from the sycamore
Came hard on a cracking bough,
The sound of somebody falling down
Still haunts my feelings now.
Joanne crashed down from the tallest branch
And she bounced from bough to twig,
And landed heavily on the ground,
Joanne was not that big.

She lay so still as if in repose
On a pile of golden leaves,
Her eyelids fluttered, and then she uttered,
'You'd best take care of these.'
And in her palm two unbroken eggs
That she'd saved as she fell down,
And screamed just once, like a little queen
That lay with a broken crown.

That was the end of our Rookwood Nights
We were made to stay inside,
We got the blame for the tragedy,
On the night that Joanne had died.
I still have those unbroken eggs
Which I blew, and kept apart,
Reminding me of that little girl
Who had thrilled a young boy's heart.

Annabelle Peak

She ambled home in her muslin dress
By the short cut through the park,
Just as the sun was sinking down
And spreading a swathe of dark,
She knew she shouldn't have tarried there
In the dying rays of the sun,
But though alarm had maddened her stare
She wouldn't give in, and run.

The Moon rose slowly over the trees
And gave out a pallid light,
Forming shadows that stretched at ease
To contribute to her fright,
The wind was soughing over her head
Where the branches groaned and creaked,
And whispered, 'Everyone else is dead,
You're the last one, Annabelle Peak.'

She whimpered there as the shadows slid
Surrounding her tiny form,
She turned then, looking behind, she did,
And clutched at her dress, forlorn,
Behind her nothing but darkness there
And then but a snapping twig,
Her frightened voice in a deep despair
Called out, 'Is that you, Rick?'

She thought she heard a chuckling sound
From the old oak tree in the dark,
But realised it was groans and sighs
From all the trees in the park,
She found her way to the cobblestones
Of her dark and eerie street,
There wasn't a sound of movement there,
Just the pat of her aching feet.

There wasn't a single gas lamp on,
Of life, there wasn't a sign,
Annabelle found her own front gate
And thought, 'I hope that it's mine.'
She tripped and fell, hitting her head
On the post as the gate had creaked,
And whispered, 'Everyone else is dead,
You're the last one, Annabelle Peak.'

Blarney

The bar of the Irish Arms was dim
On that cold, wet Wednesday night,
Was lit with guttering candles where
Was once electric light,
I'd gone to visit O'Bryan there
He was perched upon his stool,
And true to form, was jabbering where
He liked to play the fool.

'Go get away wi' yer blarney,' said
Old Jim from County Down,
He'd always paid O'Bryan out
When O'Bryan was in town,
'The little people will fix you, Jim,'
O'Bryan said, and cursed,
'They'll put your tyres on backwards,
Set you spinning in reverse.'

'You and your Leprechauns,' said Jim,
And then he almost choked,
As sparks of blue and flashes then
Erupted from his throat,
'Oh hell, he'll blame the beer,' the stocky
Barman then had cried,
'He's always blaming something,'
Said O'Bryan, 'but he lied.'

And all the while old Jim had stood
As if he was transfixed,
As little sparks of lightning flowed
From beer to fingertips,
'I think his spring has sprung,' the stocky
Barman then opined,
'I blame that new repairman,
Otherwise, I wouldn't mind.'

I noticed that O'Bryan was looking
Green around the gills,
But pointing to his empty glass
And calling for refills,
Then when he turned to talk to me
I heard a sudden clunk,
His eyes had popped, his jaw had dropped,
And something, somewhere stunk.

O'Bryan's Colleen then had thrust
Her head inside the bar,
'Come on old man, I'm waiting
In the yard, I've got the car.'
But he stood still and frozen with
A whirring little sound,
That came from in his trousers,
Sparked his shoes, and ran to ground.

'I blame myself,' said Colleen with
A coy and cheeky grin,
'The day that that repairman said
That I should trade him in.
Half the town are robots, in the
Streets and in the parks.'
I left the Irish Arms that night
And checked myself for sparks.

Days Gone By

When I look back, my mind fills up
With seasons of heat and snow,
With Autumn leaves and a sense that grieves
For Spring - where did it go?
From birth, the seasons will tumble on
With little time for respite,
The days and weeks, they sing their song
Whether it's day or night.

Like the constant drip of a faulty tap
Time slips away from our grasp,
It trickles on through our fingertips
Like the sand in an hour glass.
Our mirror images shift and change
Just as we're walking by,
Like drifting clouds, and the driving rain
Out of a clear blue sky.

And you, my darling, are not immune
To the movement of time and tide,
So take your seat up beside me, dear,
On our magic carpet ride.
Each day is part of our history
That we've lived with love and care,
So though the end is a mystery
We shall meet each other there.

Black and Whites

The longer the years roll on ahead
The more I live in the past,
Dreading the day that I'll be dead
No longer part of the cast.
The best of the years have come and gone
But live in my memory,
Whenever a song, or favourite tune
Comes wafting across to me.

For then strange figures, risen like ghosts
Erupt from my black and whites,
The photo album, tattered and torn
Slips out of my hands at night.
And then I sleep, and I dream of those
Who once were part of my day,
But drifted into my past somehow
To where? But no-one can say.

All that joy, and the laughter spent
An echo of times gone by,
Dispersed, along with the ghosts that went
Their way, to wither and die.
And though I often conjure a name
From out of the who knows where,
All I get is a flash of eyes,
A smile, a bundle of hair.

I wonder if anyone thinks of me
As part of their long, dead past,
And muses if I'm alive or free
From the chains of life, at last.
Whatever happened to all that love
That we spent, that drifted away?
Does it float around in the atmosphere
To hold us again, some day?

For love once flowed like a mountain stream
In the years that flashed on by,
Love was the hope that we thought to dream
That made us both laugh and cry,
Love that we lost caused bitter tears
That fell on the parched, dry ground,
And love it was, that swelled in our hearts,
That love, the love that we found.

The Worst Day

The weather was cold and bleak that day
A rumble up in the skies,
The Moon had only been put to bed
After a slow sunrise,
I shivered at the chill in the air
And looked for a sign of rain,
Not knowing that particular day
Was going to bring me pain.

Each day will follow the day before
And nothing will seem to change,
We wake, and follow the same old road,
With nothing to rearrange.
The planets spin as they always do,
The earth revolves round the sun,
And life goes on in its dreary round
As it does for everyone.

But certain days will stand out in time
They're never the also-rans,
And this began with a telephone call
Like the rattle of garbage cans,
I should have known that an early call
As this, would herald the ides,
A lifelong shift that would ebb and drift
As long as the sea had tides.

But first was an echoing silence
Like a seashell, locked in the line,
Giving a sense of foreboding
That was wilful, meant by design,
The voice was cold, and my heart was chilled
And I hoped that its words had lied,
As the whole of the universe stood still
On the day that my father died.

The Soldier

She cried sad tears as she packed his bag,
'But I'll be back in the Spring,
So dry your tears and kiss me now
Don't worry about a thing.'
She waved him off as he strode away
And she closed the oaken door,
While thunderclouds swirled round his head
As he went away to war.

They said it would only last six months
That the war was almost won,
While they sat safe at home to plan
As they slaughtered everyone.
They kept a regular body count
And they said, 'We're doing well,
They're only killing five of us
For the ten we send to hell.'

The winter came on quickly and
The roads were snow and ice,
It froze the caterpillar tracks
And the troops were fed on rice,
Their hands and feet were blue with cold
As the frostbite took its toll,
And men who'd been young boys before
Were suddenly looking old.

That six months had become a year
And there seemed to be no end,
His wife still hadn't heard from him
So she went to find a friend,
While he clung on to her picture
Safe and warm in his battledress,
She very rarely thought of him
And as time went, less and less.

The year became first two, then three,
As the enemy dug in,
The trenches filled with mud and blood
As the guns boomed out their din,
His friends fell slowly one by one
With a last and timely curse,
While he despaired of his wife at home
Could the war be getting worse?

But she was wooed by a bureaucrat
Who had kept his fingers clean,
He won her heart with his friendly chat
And his war was pink champagne,
Her memories were fading away
Of her man who strode to war,
And now he seemed to have disappeared
She was wondering, 'What for?'

The war was into its fifth year when
A man came limping home,
He'd lost one leg beneath the knee
And a crutch was all he owned,
He met his wife at the open door
And she said, 'You can't come in.
There's too much water under the bridge,'
And a man was blocking him.

Her picture suddenly fluttered out
From deep in his battledress,
'I see, while I've been loving you more,
Then you've been loving me less.'
Her man then tried to shoo him away
Till the soldier, in surprise,
Brought the war to the bureaucrat
With a bullet between his eyes.

Winding the Clock

When father put on his starched white shirt
His collar, buttoned to creak,
Then fixed his tie and his black top hat,
It meant the end of the week.
He'd line us up in the living room
And tell our mother to stop,
To join us there with her whisking broom
To watch him winding the clock.

He'd check the time with his pocket watch
Then pull out the old brass key,
Open the glass on the mantle clock
Then turn, and grimace at me.
'The clock is two minutes slow this week,
So what do you say to that?'
'It must have been Jonathon Slack,' I'd squeak,
And shiver, under my hat.

'A hundred and twenty seconds gone,'
He'd turn and say to his wife,
'A whole two minutes, stolen from us,
There's not enough time in life.'
So she would turn with her whisking broom
And whisk them out of the door,
A hundred and twenty seconds gone
Would never be heard of more.

Then he would turn and advance the clock
And wind it up with the key,
'If I catch up with Jonathon Slack
Then he'll have to deal with me.
If I should catch him a-slink round here
I'll beat him up with a stick,
Sixty for every tock he took,
And sixty for every tick.'

We didn't know he was raving mad
Till they came and locked him up,
And I would visit him once a week
And take his favourite cup.
Before I left, he'd give me the key,
Say, 'tell your mother to stop,
And whisk the missing seconds away
While you are winding the clock.'

Fy Mam

You left me alone one afternoon
Nursing a loving scar,
But never you thought to warn, from you
To me, wherever you are.
You slipped through the walls of the Nursing Home
Like a Sylph, intent on escape,
Chuckling at your freedom, clad
In an old Welsh bonnet and cape.

You flew in the blue Australian sky
And you went off looking for Wales,
The land of your own forefathers
Sat in their pubs, and drinking their ales.
You looked for the old Welsh miners
Listened for songs that ended their shift,
But found in the silent Rhondda
Only the ghosts of time in its drift.

The echoes of Men of Harlech
Sit in your mind, from back in your youth,
A world full of soot and coal dust,
And a young girl just looking for truth.
All of your younger siblings
Gone on ahead, but waiting for you,
And asking that vital question
Where did you go, and what did you do?

You brought up your loving children
Under the hot Australian sun,
But never cast off your Welshness,
Sang in your lilt to charm everyone.
You wrote us your children's stories
Read us to bed, and gave us delight,
Of all of the gifts you gave us
Mine was the best, you taught me to write.

Dream Sequence

We'd been at sea for a month, I dreamed,
But never away from land,
It always lay in the distance there
A vista of sea and sand,
While you would stand at the tossing prow
And stare at it, more and more,
And cry and whine at me all the time
Till I pulled in again, to shore.

I didn't like what I saw out there
The beach was a seaweed slime,
But you jumped out, and you turned about
And called to me all the time.
'Come follow me, or you love me not,'
You cried in the sharp salt air,
'How could you doubt,' I started to shout,
'I follow you everywhere.'

You clambered over the rocky beach
While I stayed back on the yacht,
You disappeared in the shade of trees
I called, 'You coming, or not?'
An eerie silence fell on the land
I thought I'd lost you for good,
I shaded my eyes with either hand
As I looked for you, in the wood.

I woke with a sudden start to see
That you had gone from our bed,
And left a note you'd written to me
'I thought I'd go on ahead.'
My heart stood still in the shade of trees
That grew up out of the mud,
And down the stairs I followed your trail,
That ominous trail of blood.

The Bet

We'd set up the bet between us,
She'd said that she loved us both,
He, one of the two-pot screamers,
While I could but plight my troth,
We'd race over town and country,
We'd follow our every urge,
To speed to the arms of Venus,
And meet her in Meckelenberg.

I hastened myself to the horses,
While he drank a further jar,
He said that he knew many courses,
Would catch me, though ever so far,
But I rode away through the marshes,
While hiding my trail through the reeds,
Where Caesar and Pompey led marches,
In fighting for Rome and its creeds.

To him, she was merely Jemima,
To me, she was Helen of Troy,
I thought that my love would remind her
That his were the whims of a boy,
I galloped in haste through the meadows,
Pursuing this vision in lace,
Who rode on ahead in a carriage
While veiling her beautiful face.

He finally caught me at Essen,
We stayed at the Getaway Inn,
I thought I would teach him a lesson,
While he had a drink for his sin,
I left while the Moon was still rising
With him reeling drunk on the floor,
To speed to the arms of my darling,
And prove that I wanted her more.

Her carriage was sat in the courtyard,
I knew I would find her within,
She smiled when she saw me arriving,
But asked, 'what has happened to him?'
I said, 'He's seduced by the bottle,
He'll always fall foul to his urge,'
She reached out her hand, and she kissed me,
'You've won me at Meckelenberg.'

The Ruling

He sat at the Council of Elders,
And frowned at the other ones there,
They'd gathered themselves all together,
To consider a case of despair,
He rarely had truck with compassion,
His eye was as sharp as a flint,
While others smiled sometimes at passion,
He didn't, not even a glint.

'They're young, and their hearts are untainted,'
Said Vinnius, wiping a tear,
'A love such as this should be feted,
We really should not interfere.'
'What nonsense,' then Termagent stated,
His eye firmly fixed on the clock,
'If this was allowed, unabated,
They'd all be out, running amok.'

'I tend to agree,' was the statement
Of hard hearted Romulus Jules,
'We can't let the human condition
Be haphazard, run without rules.
They both think that life is before them,
Is joyful and fancy and free,
Don't know that fortune might ignore them,
By granting them dire poverty.'

'How could you all be so hard hearted,'
Said Gladdius then, with a sigh,
'Has your vision of life become sordid,
And if so, are you wondering why?
Don't you ever think back and remember
How you felt at the blush of a cheek,
How you knelt at her breast in September,
And her kiss was the goal you would seek?'

'She will leave him one day, broken hearted,
And what will become of him then,
He will wish that love never had started
And reap the full sadness of men.'
'But he may prove his love to Giselda,
And she'll cleave to him, never to roam,'
So they voted, the Council of Elders,
And that vote was to leave them alone.

The Grimoire

While I sat pondering in my chair
One dark and scabrous evening,
With chills and damp spreading everywhere
From the Grimoire I was reading,
I found a spell there for raising hell
In a strange and ancient cursive,
In ink so red that it must have bled
With a fungus on the surface.

I found the wording so curious
That I studied and absorbed it,
It made me shiver and shake until
My mind was more than torpid.
I couldn't feel and I couldn't move
In the darkness all around me,
I must have seemed like a corpse, just then,
If anyone had found me.

All feeling seemed to have slipped away
As I sat there, full of tension,
I would, if I could have thought, to pray
But it came to my attention
That something hovered above my chair
And flapped about above me,
A thought of death with such evil breath
That I knew it couldn't love me.

'What evil troll is above my chair,'
I whispered, almost choking,
I felt it crackling through my hair
Like a fire it was stoking.
I caught a glimpse of a flapping rag
That hovered, just behind me,
But couldn't turn, and for that I'm glad
For I feared the thing would blind me.

A hand reached over my shoulder then
Of fingers, mere phalanges,
There was no skin, but I felt the sin
That a sense of fear enhances,
The fingers pointed along the script
Of the Grimoire, laid before me,
And showed me some of the hell within
As part of the devil's story.

I never sat in that chair again
In such cold and scabrous weather,
But try to stay in the world of men
With that Grimoire closed forever.
Whatever's hiding behind that chair
I can feel its presence, hating,
To try me out on a do or dare,
It will be forever waiting.

Death of The Cormorant

The clouds were dark and billowing
Over a wild and fretful sea,
Just where the old barque 'Cormorant'
Went down in '83,
The waves were crashing over the rocks
That had ripped its hull apart,
Back in the days of sailing ships
It had torn its wooden heart.

I sat and watched as the rain came down
And I tried to visualise,
That final death ship plunging where
The horizon met my eyes,
For I knew out there on the after deck
Clung a maiden in distress,
Who sailed to shore for her wedding
Dressed in a pale grey muslin dress.

She held on hard to the lanyards
As the sails came crashing down,
The masts and all their rigging
Tangled and torn, a tearing sound,
But over the rage of wind and storm
They could hear her plaintive cry,
'My sisters all were married, happily,
Why, Oh Lord, can't I?'

But then the storm had settled in
And I sat beneath a cliff,
Sheltering from the driving hail
To contemplate, 'What if?'
What if the girl had swum to shore
As the ship was breaking down,
I'd not be what I thought was me
If that girl had come to town.

My grandfather stood by that cliff
As he watched it break apart,
That barque they called the 'Cormorant'
That carried his aching heart,
He would have married that plaintive girl
If she had survived the shock,
Of being dashed and smashed ashore
On some uncaring rock.

Instead he married a servant girl
When his life had settled down,
And buried the love he'd truly lost
From the 'Cormorant', who drowned.
And as I sat there in the storm
I fancied I heard a cry,
'My sisters all were married, happily,
Why, Oh Lord, can't I?'

The Thousand Nights

Where does this story start, I thought,
Before picking up my pen,
It had to do with that lamp I bought
In that antique shop, back when.
The lamp, it was quaint and curious
And sealed with a Chinese glyph,
I couldn't but help see magic there
With the faint thought of 'What if?'

It might have been like Aladdin's lamp
In that tale of a thousand nights,
That Chinese pauper and ne'er do well
Who set everything to rights,
He'd had to use the sorcerer's ring
To reclaim the lamp once more,
And though the lamp was a battered thing
I set it down on the floor.

I noticed some oil was still within
When I opened the top to see,
And in the oil was a silver ring
To add to the mystery,
I tried it on and I rubbed the lamp
Where it sat, down on the floor,
When suddenly there was someone knocking,
Knocking at my front door.

I opened up and a woman stood
Wrapped up in an eastern veil,
She said that her name was Scheherazade,
And then she began to wail,
'I know that you have taken the lamp,
The lamp that is surely mine,
I'll give you twice what you paid for it,
If only you'd be so kind.'

'There isn't a chance,' I answered her,
'I paid for it, fair and square,
It isn't for sale.' She started to wail,
And tore at her long, dark hair,
'I'm tied to the lamp for a thousand nights,
You'll have to put up with me,
Unless you sell me the Genie's lamp
I fear I'll never be free.'

So here I sit on the hundredth night
And pause to pick up my pen,
For she has told me a hundred tales
With some that I'd heard, back when.
She sits, cross legged, down on the floor
And tells of the forty thieves,
While I just sit and tear at my hair,
In hopes that she ups and leaves.

Time Travel

Why do they mess our clocks about,
Turning them on, then back,
I get confused, and sometimes shout
'It seems like a time attack.'
How much light do we need at night
Before we can get to sleep,
And where is the sun when day's begun,
Below the horizon, deep.

How it destroys my body clock
When changing it twice a year,
Stumbling round in the dark one day
Till daylight will reappear.
I never catch my bus on time,
I find that it's been and gone,
Or sit down and wait, an hour late,
The world seems to carry on.

I never know when it's time to go
To play with the mantle clock,
To see if its tick is fast or slow
Or wait for the perfect tock.
Yesterday I went out the door,
Discovered an empty street,
There wasn't a moving body there,
Not even the sound of feet.

But out in the road an old man stood
A man with a long white beard,
He seemed to be sweeping the footpath in
The rest of it disappeared.
And only half of the houses stood
Where once they'd stood in a row,
And in the distance an open space
So white that it looked like snow.

He saw me stop with an open mouth,
And his face turned into a grin,
'There's always one,' he chuckled aloud,
'I think you should go back in.'
I stood bemused as the clouds above
Swept over just half a sky,
'I think that I must be going mad,'
I said, then muttering 'Why?'

'I don't have time to listen to you,
There's too much work to begin,
If you don't know what's happened to you,
I think you should go back in.
I'll bet you just put forward your clock
Instead of turning it back,
You're now two hours ahead of your time,
And everything's out of whack.

It took him hours to rebuild the town
In time for the morning bus,
He wasn't one of our human kind,
He couldn't be one of us.
I went back in and reversed the clock
And tried to settle my mind,
But never again will advance the clock
At the end of our summertime.

Also available from Lulu.com
And by the same author
The following Novels and Poetry

Novels:
Cates's Creek
The Afterdeath
Prittik's Will
Experiment in Fear
The Sumner Tontine
Blackrock Island
Heaven's Ridge
Dark Harbour

Novellas:
London Bridge is falling down
The Legacy of Zion Stark
When Lightning Strikes Twice
Trafalgar
To Die For
The Hangman

Humour:
Tales of Wudgi Crossing

Experience:
Arrows from Wenzhou

Poems:
Pen & Ink, the Complete Works 1968-2008

Narrative Poetry:

Timepieces – Poems Out of Time and Other Places
At Journey's End – Narrative Poems Vol. II
The Demon Horse on the Carousel – and other Gothic Delights.
Poems of Myth and Scare
The Devil on the Tree – and other poems of Dysfunction.
Tales from the Magi
Taking Root
The Storm and the Tall Ship Pier
The Book on the Topmost Shelf
Tall Tales for Tired Times – T.T.T.T.
Butterflies
The Widow of Martin Black
Goblin Dell
The Mind Catcher
The Angel of Lygon Street
The Obelisk
The Season of the Witch
Smugglers Pie
The Red Knight
My China
Warlock Park

Lulu.com/spotlight/David Lewis Paget

www.ingramcontent.com/pod-product-compliance
Lightning Source LLC
Chambersburg PA
CBHW061655040426
42446CB00010B/1746